Presentation Skills for Scie

MW00698032

Scientists are rarely given fo
yet are often called upon to p
book provides a practical guide .. ..a...a. ...a ...a ...very of scientific presentations, whatever the topic. Its practical "how-to" style leaves
discussion of the background psychology of public speaking to others
and focuses instead on the issues that are of immediate concern to the
busy scientist. The text covers all of the important aspects of scientific
presentations, ranging from audience awareness to handling questions.
Links are included throughout the text to the accompanying DVD, which
contains annotated video clips of speakers delivering a talk, and demon-
strates the common problems found with many presenters, as well as
the exercises designed to overcome them. Image files of different slide
layouts, colour schemes and font styles demonstrate the design issues
that one must consider when creating visual material.

Edward Zanders is Managing Director of ScienceInform Ltd, a training
company for people involved with the research-based pharmaceutical
and biotechnology industries. He has over thirty years' experience as a
biomedical research scientist in both academia and industry.

Lindsay MacLeod is a highly experienced London tourist guide, and
taught presentation skills to London Blue Badge guides for fifteen years.
She is a member of the Institute of Tourist Guiding, the government
approved body that sets standards for tourist guides.

Presentation Skills for Scientists
A Practical Guide

Edward Zanders
ScienceInform Ltd

Lindsay MacLeod
Lindsay MacLeod Ltd

CAMBRIDGE
UNIVERSITY PRESS

CAMBRIDGE UNIVERSITY PRESS
Cambridge, New York, Melbourne, Madrid, Cape Town, Singapore,
São Paulo, Delhi, Dubai, Tokyo

Cambridge University Press
The Edinburgh Building, Cambridge CB2 8RU, UK

Published in the United States of America by Cambridge University Press, New York

www.cambridge.org
Information on this title: www.cambridge.org/9780521741033

First published 2010

Printed in the United Kingdom at the University Press, Cambridge

A catalogue record for this publication is available from the British Library

Library of Congress Cataloguing in Publication data
Zanders, Edward D.
Presentation skills for scientists : a practical guide / Edward Zanders, Lindsay MacLeod.
   p. cm.
Includes bibliographical references and index.
ISBN 978-0-521-74103-3 (pbk.)
1. Communication in science.   2. Public speaking.   3. Scientists – Vocational guidance.
I. MacLeod, Lindsay.   II. Title.
Q223.Z36   2010
808'.0665 – dc22   2009038170

ISBN 978-0-521-74103-3 Paperback

Contents

Preface   *page* vii

Acknowledgements   ix

Introduction   x

The presentation flowchart   xii

1   Audience   1

2   Planning the talk   6

3   Selection and assembly of visual material   13

4   Controlling nerves   23

5   Voice   31

6   Delivery   39

7   Science and the English language   48

8   Handling questions   55

9   How did it go?   61

Conference checklist   64

Further reading   65

Index   66

Preface

If surveys are to be believed, for most people formal public speaking is worse than bereavement; literally a fate worse than death. Pity then the practising scientists who have to plan and execute complex experiments, interpret the results, write them up for publication and then talk about them and answer questions in front of their peers. There is no choice in the matter, so they have to be able to plan a presentation, design their own visual material, speak clearly and confidently and be in control. Some people enjoy this challenge and have an instinctive ability to communicate information to audiences. Others find this particularly daunting and let themselves down through nervousness, poor voice control or by producing confusing slides that fail to convey a clear message. Most scientists know if they belong to the second group of people and most do want to improve their performance. This improvement can be achieved by every speaker, regardless of personality, but requires practice and attention to detail. The result will be a more confident speaker who can convey enthusiasm and authority without necessarily having an extrovert personality.

This book and associated DVD-ROM are designed as a practical guide to scientific presentation that busy scientists can refer to without having to absorb large amounts of theory and background to verbal communication. It is based on a course that we have delivered to technicians, PhD students, postdoctoral fellows and business development managers in Cambridge and elsewhere in the United Kingdom. Apart from receiving instruction in preparing and delivering scientific talks, each delegate is filmed delivering a short technical presentation and the recording is played back to them. Over the years we have learnt a great deal about the specific problems with scientific presentation and how these problems can be addressed. We therefore decided to pass this knowledge on to others in the form of this book and the DVD-ROM that contains realistic presentation scenarios and helpful exercises.

The authors have used their different professional backgrounds in a complementary way; Lindsay MacLeod covers the "soft skills" required for all public speaking, drawing on her many years of experience in training Blue Badge guides in London, and over twenty years of regular presenting. Ed Zanders covers the skills required to process and deliver scientific data to an audience in a short period of time. He brings over thirty years' experience as a practising scientist and has studied many hundreds of presentations from junior scientists up to Nobel Laureates; he has also delivered many of his own talks in the UK and abroad.

The book is presented in a compact format, enabling the speaker to carry it in a case or handbag, perhaps en route to a conference or seminar venue; the enclosed DVD-ROM can even be used on the road or at the conference. We envisage this being particularly useful for last-minute practice of the exercises to control nerves and enhance vocal modulation.

The chapters are laid out as components of a flowchart to cover the most important aspects of scientific presentation systematically, ranging from audience awareness through to handling questions. Although the text can be referred to on its own, the material on the DVD-ROM provides detailed practical help in the form of slides and video clips and is a critical part of the publication. The DVD-ROM includes a PowerPoint presentation on a biomedical topic to illustrate effective and poor delivery styles for native and non-native English speakers. It also includes demonstrations of exercises designed to assist in developing a clear modulated speaking style. Finally, we have included a checklist at the end of the book covering the key points that have to be addressed before giving a presentation.

Acknowledgements

Thanks are due to Sian Deciantis and her colleagues at Nexus TV in Cambridge UK for filming and editing the DVD-ROM material. We also thank the three presenters David Evans, Ardian Kastrati and Jennifer MacLeod for their cheerful willingness to devote time to the project and to deal with unfamiliar technical material.

We acknowledge Cartoonbank.com for the use of the New Yorker Cartoons in the book.

The Y chromosome figure for the slide theme example is reproduced by kind permission of Nature Publications.

We thank Professor Jane Gitschier (University of California San Francisco) who inspired the idea of creating an example talk around a fictitious gene on the Y chromosome, the OOPS gene.

Finally, we thank our families for their support and encouragement.

Introduction

Background to scientific presentation

A scientific presentation is normally a formal communication of information to an audience at a conference, seminar or laboratory meeting. The majority of talks describe the background and design of experiments to increase knowledge of a particular scientific phenomenon. Then the results of these experiments are delivered, as well as the conclusions that can be drawn from them. The conclusions drawn from these experiments and the data that support them are almost always the most important pieces of information that can be communicated to an audience of fellow scientists. Presentations are therefore a showcase for your work, or that of your institution. How well you deliver scientific information depends on a number of factors; these include control of nerves and voice, as well as creating visual media that convey information clearly in as short a time as possible.

As a scientist, you are often too busy to think about the deep-seated motivations that drive your work and the way that you present it to the outside world. Maybe you are too tied up with the exhilaration of making new discoveries; alternatively (and more frequently for most scientists), you suffer from the frustrations of failed experiments or having to deal with non-scientific issues such as raising money and dealing with lab politics. Success, when it comes, however, makes these frustrations irrelevant; the only feeling now is one of wanting to publish the results and present them at meetings. The main reward for this success is one of appreciation by one's scientific peers, be they colleagues or competitors. This is one of the main motivators of the practising scientist and must not be underestimated. It is true that other motivations exist, for example to help humanity by discovering new medicines to cure disease, but these drivers often take second place to simple curiosity and interest in solving problems. A consequence of all this is that you as a scientist are primarily interested in hard data. If you read a published paper, you want to examine the results in fine detail. If you hear a talk on a subject that is relevant to your work, you want to see the data.

Most scientists do not have the time or inclination to think about how the features that make a particular talk effective may be identified and used to advantage in their own presentations. It is, however, worth making the effort to identify your key behaviours that can be enhanced or reduced as appropriate. Such insight will lead to improvements in your own delivery and avoid your being lost in the crowd of speakers who deliver indifferent talks.

The main components of any verbal communication are delivery, speaker appearance and content. According to surveys, content makes by far the least impact on an audience. Can this really be the case for scientific presentations as well? After all, experimental data are the currency with which science operates. Perhaps it depends on the relationship between the speaker and audience. If a competitor is showing results from experiments that you have done, or were planning to do, then poor delivery and speaker appearance might not be so important; this is because all that matters now is the data. This is a familiar situation, particularly for the younger scientist who is under pressure to publish original experimental work. The adrenalin flows, not just in the speaker, but in the recipient who is anxious not to be scooped, or has been given exciting new ideas to explore. This is not, however, a recommendation to ignore delivery and presentation. A seminar describing a major new finding in immunology comes to mind; the data kept the audience engrossed, but also agitated, as the speaker was monotonous and boring. In fact, these last aspects remain in the memory for nearly three decades, long after the data were forgotten!

The presentation flowchart

The following flowchart covers the key elements of a scientific presentation.

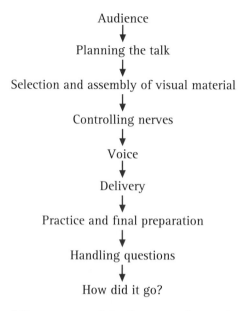

If you want to deliver a successful talk you need to review each chapter thoroughly (and the DVD-ROM material) so you can answer the following questions:

Is the material

    Tailored to the right audience?
    Well constructed with a clear theme and take-home message?
    Supported with clear visual material?
    Delivered clearly without nervous distractions?

Are the questions handled professionally?

A note on using the DVD-ROM

The following chapters contain background material and basic guidelines for preparation and delivery of scientific talks. The DVD-ROM that comes with the book contains video, text and images designed to illustrate specific topics and to provide exercises for controlling nerves and enhancing delivery. We have placed the *DVD-ROM* logo in the text where there is relevant material on the disc and have specified the files that can be accessed through the main menu.

1 Audience

"Whew! Tough crowd."

This chapter highlights key points about the audience that need to be considered before you attempt to plan the presentation in detail; it also gives guidance on how to overcome the first sign of nervousness resulting from anticipation of who might be coming to hear you speak.

Understanding what audiences expect

When planning a scientific presentation, it is worth thinking about audience expectations from the outset. If you empathise with them, you will ensure that the way you construct and deliver your talk will satisfy their needs and avoid creating antagonism towards you.

> **!** Audiences have a fixed idea of the time allotted to a talk and will rarely tolerate a time overrun.

Plan to keep within a specified time by controlling the number of slides used, and by rehearsing the talk.

Imagine yourself listening to your own talk

This introduces the idea of a presentation as a selling exercise. Successful marketing is based on finding out what the customer wants and identifying benefits for them. Just trying to sell what you think the customer ought to want rarely works. So if you put yourself in the shoes of the audience you will be able to tune your talk to their needs and interests. This requires some research beforehand. If you are invited to give a seminar at another institution, you should find out something about the department or company that you will be visiting and tailor your talk accordingly. Similarly for conferences, a review of the programme will help you to present your talk in the correct context for the audience. For example, there may be several presentations that cover the same subject material, so there is a danger of the introductions from each different speaker saying the same thing. In this case, a different way of looking at the subject background would break the monotony and keep the audience alert.

Your target audience

Who will be in the audience for your talk – in other words, who is the talk aimed at?

Most scientists give their first presentation to colleagues as part of their graduate education, then move on to reporting the results of their work at internal lab meetings. Over the course of their subsequent careers they will be asked to speak at short conference or workshop sessions, formal seminars and to contribute keynote conference speeches (generally in that order).

Each of the above stages form part of an apprenticeship in public speaking requiring, among other things, a sense of the particular needs of each audience. Most of your audiences will be scientists working on similar problems to you; a significant number will have a specialist interest in your work as colleagues or competitors. You may occasionally need to deliver a talk to scientists from totally different disciplines or an audience without any science training at all. Although every one of the above scenarios requires a common standard of presentation and clarity of content, there will obviously need to be a change in emphasis between background material and the research findings.

A specialist audience does not want a long introduction to what they know already and will be eagerly awaiting the data. Since the specialists are likely to be well acquainted with the experimental techniques under discussion, they will probably have strong views about the conclusions drawn from the findings presented. All of these points drive some speakers to make their talks as complex as possible in order to impress their peers, as well as to build a defensive shield against attack. They fire off an unstructured barrage of figures and complex diagrams and often overrun the allotted time for their presentation. The end result is a talk whose message cannot be properly evaluated, even by the experts who the speaker is trying to impress.

Good speakers can introduce a subject, even to a specialist audience, without any sense of being patronising or "dumbing down". They do not, however, commit the cardinal error in their introduction of using up too much of the time reserved for presentation of the more complex data and their interpretation.

> *A single exception to this comes to mind: a prestigious biochemist giving a one-hour seminar in a major US medical centre managed to get away with spending the first twenty minutes telling a slightly off-colour joke (something to do with his wife and photographs) totally unrelated to his subject. He then proceeded to dazzle the audience for the remainder of the time with a well-crafted presentation. Although entertaining, we would most certainly not recommend this approach!*

Increase the complexity of your material seamlessly as you move into the main body of the talk allowing everyone to keep up. As with all presentations, variety adds interest, so there will be situations in which a more dramatic introduction may be more appropriate to capture and hold the attention of the audience.

! Think of the talk as a flight in an airplane: taxi gently, then make a rapid but smooth takeoff, spend most of the time at cruising altitude, then gently descend and land.

! If you scan the audience and find some looking bored, distracted or even asleep, you and your talk may not be at fault.

Some may have personal problems that take their mind off science, have suffered from lack of sleep (after a conference social event perhaps?) or may simply look that way even when they're interested. Ignore these intrusions into your train of thought and don't let them distract you from your talk.

> *One department head used to sit in the front row and feign sleep during seminars to deliberately play games with the speaker. He would then "wake up" at the end and ask some highly effective questions – luckily, most speakers were aware of this beforehand.*

Should I worry about who will be in the audience?

A major source of anticipatory nervousness in a speaker is the thought of who might be in the audience for their talk. One of the most common fears arises from having to present in front of friends and work colleagues, as opposed to complete strangers. Presumably they fear the stigma of self-humiliation in front of people who will be around them for a long time after the talk has ended. At least they will probably never see the strangers again.

The techniques described in detail in Chapter 4 – "Controlling nerves" and on the DVD-ROM will help to control this common problem with audiences.

One particular fear (raised frequently by delegates attending our courses) is that of speaking in front of distinguished experts in the audience. This "seniority perception" anxiety is largely due to lack of confidence in the speaker's own knowledge and ability, and the fear of being exposed by ruthless questioning. Although the latter point is covered in the "Handling questions" chapter and on the DVD-ROM, "seniority perception" anxiety as a specific problem is discussed in the following paragraphs.

Presenting can be daunting to scientists at the early stages of their careers. One reason is because they are afraid of making a bad impression on senior people in the audience who may have a direct influence on their future employment. This is a natural response, particularly if you are faced with a Nobel Laureate, or equivalent, in the seminar audience. Even the accomplished physicist Richard Feynman was taken aback before delivering a seminar at Princeton as a young man, when Albert Einstein arrived quietly and sat down in the front row.

Nervousness of this type is of course all in the mind. It follows that a change in thinking from negative to positive is required to control it from the outset.

Realise that you should know more about your own data than anyone else

Senior people might be more interested in the science than in you in particular. They will judge the material by the same standards as everyone else, so it is up to you to be as rigorous as possible in your coverage of new data and its interpretation.

Sometimes the presence of audience members with a political agenda can create problems. They may be scientists who are using you as a proxy to fight a war with your supervisor and will be deliberately critical of your talk. The only way to deal with this and "seniority perception" anxiety is to adhere to the following:

| ! | Make sure the talk is interesting, informative and runs to time. |

| ! | Make sure that you know your material. |

In this way, you will bring the majority of the audience on to your side, probably including the senior people, and in doing so will isolate any individual with a different agenda.

Preparation is all!

A colleague once told the story of how a relatively junior scientist gave a sloppy presentation at an international conference and was humiliated by a major scientific figure with the words "my dear boy, this field is hard enough for the professionals, let alone amateurs". This nightmare scenario was brought about (although the response was unnecessarily harsh), by not caring about the audience and its needs.

2 Planning the talk

"It's plotted out. I just have to write it."

This chapter covers the process of scoping out a presentation using a set of logical guidelines. If these are followed, along with those highlighted in subsequent chapters, the end result should be a coherent story that is delivered within the time period available for the talk (e.g. one-hour seminar or fifteen-minute conference talk).

The time constraint: cutting the cloth to fit

Before getting into detail about the preparation of the talk itself, we must stress the need to keep it within a defined time limit. This (and many other points raised in this book) may seem obvious and almost unworthy of comment, but it still amazes us how so many of our course delegates give their prepared talk with far more slides than could ever be presented within the allotted time. This of course applies to speakers doing a talk for real, including many who should be experienced enough to know better.

For the purposes of this chapter and the next on selection of material, we define "slides" as units of visual material displayed to the audience. These will be mainly digital slides created using PowerPoint software, but there will be circumstances where a chalkboard, flipchart or overhead projector will be used instead. In these cases, the time taken to draw on the board/chart (or even laying out the overhead by hand) will slow the talk down compared to when digital slides are used.

> **!** Determine the maximum number of slides that can be comfortably delivered within the allotted time.

The following table gives a rough guide for different types of presentation based on an average slide rate of slightly less than one per minute. These figures do not have to be adhered to exactly, of course. Some slides can be lingered over for most of the talk, so the actual number used might be very low. Alternatively, filler slides may be used to break the talk into logical sections and may last for much less than a minute, so the final number may even exceed the maximum quoted. Common sense must prevail – the number must realistically match the time available for the talk.

Type of talk	Duration (minutes)	Time for questions (minutes)	Suggested working number of slides
Conference/ workshop session	10	5	7–9
Formal seminar	45–50	10–15	30–40
Keynote speech	30	0–10	20–25
Business presentation[a]	60 maximum	Ad hoc	<20

[a] The business presentation may involve a description of the presenter's company, key personnel and technology. These meetings nearly always stimulate questions throughout the talk, thus derailing any plans for keeping to time. Since time is in short supply for busy executives, it pays to keep the presentation as succinct as possible. A solution is to incorporate fewer slides than would normally be the case for a conference or seminar session of this length.

This thinking also applies to internal lab meetings, where the data will be subjected to detailed probing by the lab head and rest of the group. Time overruns annoy these people because the lab meetings are normally held first thing in the morning, or at lunchtime, so they get anxious to return to their experiments while there is enough time left in the day.

Turning your material into a story

A dry recitation of facts does not make a good talk. Since science deals with facts, there is a real danger that presenters will fall into this trap. It also occurs in areas outside science, including tourism. Who has not been bored by a poorly trained guide who just lists dates and places without any context or human interest? This is why crafting the talk into a story is of fundamental importance. We don't of course expect scientific talks to be works of fiction (despite some high-profile cases of just that in the last few years). The story format conveys the key message (or messages) in a way that human beings can absorb. Many speakers do not think in this way from the outset, so the resulting talk can be formulaic and boring.

> **!** Identify the key message you want to convey and build the talk around it.

The ability to abstract the key message from a collection of research material is directly related to the degree of understanding of the research itself and why it was performed in the first place. A presenter should be able to summarise the essence of their work in one or two sentences. Obviously this process will exclude subtle nuances and complexities, but it is not designed for that. It is a thinking exercise that forces the speaker to move away from the fine detail to a higher-level view of the material. Employ this at the planning phase to create a framework on which to build your talk.

In 1993, a request was made to the Science Minister in the British Government to contribute money towards developing the Large Hadron Collider, a machine designed in part to prove the existence of the Higgs Boson. The Minister (a history graduate) then asked the physics community to provide, on a single A4 sheet of paper, a description of the Higgs theory and why it was important. Five winning entries were received, including an analogy comparing the Higgs field to a cocktail party with Prime Minister Margaret Thatcher as the guest of honour. Although the story is quite entertaining, there is a clear lesson here about reducing huge complexity to a relatively simple description; furthermore, the use of analogy to convey the key message is a powerful tool for the presenter and is effective with both specialist and lay audiences.

Structuring the talk

The basic structure of the talk needs boundaries so that you can guide the audience in whatever direction you want. The route and destination must be planned carefully, otherwise the audience will be lost and the talk will be a failure. Once you have defined the limits of the talk (number of slides and so on) and articulated the key message, the next stage involves establishing a logical sequence.

There seems to be a good consensus among writers on scientific presentation about just what that logical sequence should be. We like the succinct version offered by the late Vernon Booth in his book *Communicating in Science* (see *Further reading*):

Why you did this work
How you did it
What you found
What you think it means.

WHY YOU DID THIS WORK

Scientists have a habit of asking questions; it's fundamental to their profession – "How does this work?", "What is the nature of this phenomenon?" and "Why does X operate and Y doesn't?" This habit lends itself naturally to scientific presentations, where a question (or series of questions) is used to guide the audience towards the key conclusions that they can take away from the talk.

> **!** Formulate a question(s) to set the talk in the right direction.

The question is normally posed after an introduction to the topic to be presented. This will be a high-level view to start with, perhaps with a historical background, or an analogy with everyday experience. If you are speaking in a conference, you could briefly relate your talk to the theme for your session to put it in context. Keep the review of the conference theme clear and brief and try to minimise the inevitable repetition that will occur with the other speakers in that session.

One of our delegates introduced his work on stereo effects in the auditory nervous system by highlighting the need for stereo hearing when crossing a busy road. This simple everyday analogy is a good example of lateral thinking that allowed the audience to immediately place his work in the right context.

HOW YOU DID IT

This is obviously similar in concept to the *Materials and Methods* section of a publication, but has to be treated carefully. Unless the experimental approach is the subject of the talk, this section should not be dwelled upon for too long. This is an area where it is tempting to list every aspect of the experimental procedure in great detail. Resist the temptation and only go into further detail if asked, either during questions, or outside the session.

WHAT YOU FOUND

This results section can prove the most challenging since there is often a need to distil a large amount of data into a form that can be presented in an intelligible way over the time available. This is possible through the use of appropriate graphics, overlays and animations. These are discussed in Chapter 3 and in the associated DVD-ROM material.

You need to use some judgement about which data are essential to support your argument; do not show every piece of data you can find because it only tires or confuses the audience. Many speakers are anxious about finishing the talk too early, or not appearing to have done enough work, and fill out the talk with totally unrealistic numbers of slides. If the maximum number of slides available is established at the outset, this should not be a problem. Of course, there may not actually be much data available, so there is more room for the introduction and conclusions, particularly a discussion of what needs to be done next.

WHAT YOU THINK IT MEANS

This concluding section must be punchy and succinct, as it could be the one thing that the audience remembers and takes away with them. This section is also the one where Summary and Conclusions often get mixed up together. The Summary lists the experimental findings that the speaker thinks are important to support the key message of the talk. This section is then followed immediately by the Conclusions section, where an interpretation of the findings is presented on a single slide.

The relative proportion of the talk that should be devoted to each of the above sections is summarised in the figure below.

Relative proportion of talk

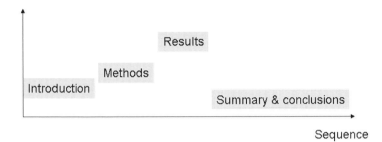

Acknowledgements

It is very rare for a speaker to have nobody to acknowledge in the collaborative world of scientific research, so colleagues should be thanked during the talk. This seems to occur most commonly at the end, after the conclusion slide has been presented, but can obscure a punchy and memorable take-home message. You could try placing acknowledgements at the beginning of the talk instead. It is common practice to show literature citations on slides, but they are often illegible. If a reference is needed to support the content of a slide, make the font legible. This, however, can distract from the rest of the slide, so it may be better to show a separate (but not too extensive) reference list.

Handling multiple themes

A short conference presentation is not long enough to cover more than one theme, so the path from question to conclusion is linear and continuous. A longer seminar or keynote speech is a different matter. The speaker may still have a single key message, but this time it can be reached by a number of paths using data that have been generated by a number of collaborators. There may also be more than one group of conclusions, so the most "punchy" should be left for the end.

The challenge with this type of presentation is to keep the key message (or messages) in focus without excessive sidetracking or stalling. The speaker must still adhere to the basic principles of storytelling, but this time with added subplots.

One example, taken from biomedical research, is the study of an experimental drug developed to treat a particular disease. This can be clearly divided into two parts. The first covers the development of the drug with reference to its target and the biology of the disease it is designed to treat. The second part describes the testing of that drug in patients and the results obtained. Both sections will have their own terminology and experimental approaches but can be made to integrate smoothly to create a coherent story (in this case with human interest, as the audience will be eagerly waiting to see if the experimental treatment works).

Natural breaks

Even if the audience is hanging on your every word during a seminar or longer talk, they will (even subconsciously) respond to a series of breaks in the flow of information. These can be brief summaries of what has been delivered already, or visual cues to introduce the next theme. There is definitely a place for appropriate humour as well, a device that is used in many thrillers to break the tension. An amusing (but relevant) cartoon can quickly lighten the mood of the audience and relax them prior to moving on to the next phase of the talk. It can also have the effect of priming the audience to your style and make them expect more of the same – even if it never arrives.

> *There are ways not to break up presentations. One of us (EZ) gave a seminar at a prestigious Boston laboratory (Nobel Laureate in audience etc.). The theme, on lymphocyte signalling, was neatly divided into two sections that could have been joined together without difficulty. He asked for questions from the audience after the first part, instead of at the end, and thus completely destroyed the momentum of the talk – a mistake he has never repeated.*

3 Selection and assembly of visual material

The Night Before the Big Meeting Frank Receives a Visit from the PowerPoint Fairy.

Visual displays are powerful tools for communicating scientific data but can be misused and cause more confusion than enlightenment. This chapter is supported by the DVD-ROM section on slide construction, and covers the main aspects of design and layout. It also describes the all-important process of presenting experimental data in a form that can be visualised and understood within a short period of time.

> **!** The speaker is the centre of attention, but should be able to direct the audience to and from the slides at will.

> **!** The slides must deliver the message that the speaker is trying to convey without confusing the audience.

It follows from these points that you as a speaker must have full control over an audience through your ability to communicate (covered in subsequent chapters) as well as control over the actual content of your presentation.

> *Very rarely, this latter control is taken away. A seminar speaker had his 35 mm slides in a projector carousel all ready to start his talk. The person who had invited him (a well-known eccentric biologist of the time) noticed a slight fault with the projector. He then proceeded to harangue the audience and eventually confiscate the projector plus slides, so the hapless speaker had no prepared material at all. Luckily, this speaker knew enough about presenting his work to be able to write the key elements on a chalkboard and save the day. Could you do that?*

General comments about visual aids

Science operates through the worldwide dissemination of experimental data, largely through the written word in peer-reviewed publications. These papers contain figures and tables that can be studied at leisure over as long a period as the reader can spare. This luxury is clearly not available to the audience listening to an oral communication, so a different approach has to be taken when preparing visual material. The data must be clearly visible to the whole audience and held just long enough (because time is at a premium) to let the information sink in.

We assume that most readers will be using digital slides based on PowerPoint software, unless the circumstances dictate otherwise (an internal lab meeting for example). Much criticism has been levelled at the digital presentation media that are now universally adopted – summarised by the phrase "death by PowerPoint". One of the main problems is the "over engineering" of the software, allowing the lazy presenter to cover up a lack of real communication with a dazzling display of visual effects. Another concern is the ubiquity of PowerPoint and the boredom engendered by having too many talks using the same style. Couldn't the same be said of the earlier use of overhead projectors and 35 mm "diazo" slides?

The reader can find more discussions on this topic in some of the books listed in *Further reading.* This phenomenon has even reached the video networking site YouTube, where there are some highly amusing spoofs on bad presentations using PowerPoint, which although exaggerated, give pause for thought to anyone who uses this software.

Given that most scientists want tools to make their lives easier and more efficient (and not spend precious time worrying about which visual format to use) it seems that PowerPoint (or equivalent) media are here to stay. This means that the software must be tamed from its wild state and the many features that it offers used selectively and appropriately.

Another aspect of visual communication in science is the sheer complexity of the material. The simplification of what were once huge technical obstacles has raised the bar for scientific publication, since more and more experiments are required by editors and referees to support a particular hypothesis to get the paper accepted. This spills over into oral communication, where the speaker and audience often have far too much material to deal with. Even the most prepared and organised speaker can struggle with the problem of how to get the key message across without oversimplification. Electronic media can help by providing builds and animations to present complex information at a rate that audiences can follow.

The world of communication is changing rapidly, with web-based interactive networks and personal digital media players becoming commonplace. These tools are already making an impact on scientific communication in the form of Pod casts, web seminars, etc. Although they will never replace the need for conventional scientific presentations, we can envisage a time when PowerPoint will just be a quaint anachronism – but that time has not yet come.

Storyboarding

"Enough storyboarding. Let's shoot something."

We assume that you have prepared the foundations for the talk according to the guidelines laid out in Chapters 1 and 2, briefly summarised below:

> **!** You have tailored the amount of background material and the level of complexity of the talk to the needs of the projected audience.

> **!** You have put a limit on the number of slides that can realistically be used in the available time.

> **!** You have established the key message that you are trying to convey as a story with flow and momentum.

> **!** You have laid out the sections from introduction to conclusions (at least in your mind).

Turning these concepts into a talk with script and a sequence of slides is not unlike the process of making a film. The whole talk (film) is laid out on a storyboard so that slides (scenes) can be easily added, removed or reordered. The storyboard itself could be written by hand on a sheet of paper or adhesive notes, or assembled electronically in the slide sorter view of PowerPoint. There is much to recommend the last method, including the ability to rapidly manipulate slides in a clear, uncluttered layout. It is also useful to be able to bring in slides from previous talks that have been archived electronically.

Set up the storyboard and bring in slides to mark out the individual elements of the storyline, i.e. introduction, methods, results, summary, conclusions. Constrain the number of slides to fit the planned length of talk (the storyboard will fill up very quickly for a short conference presentation). The slides do not have to be complete at this stage as the idea is just to establish the flow and rhythm of the talk. Decide on the design theme for the slides and keep them the same throughout to avoid a jarring effect.

Once the core layout has been established, you can start to fill in detail, regularly checking the slides in full view using the *Slide show* facility. Review each slide for relevance, legibility and clarity of message. This is the time to get rid of that slide with a terrific image but no relevance, or one that is too complex to be read at all. Equally, you might be able to bring in some fresh ideas to support your message – it's all part of the creative process. The sheer abundance of presentation material on display at conferences and seminars will help to give you the necessary inspiration (and critical judgement).

The final task is to ensure that the slides transition smoothly from start to finish without breaking the flow, unless you have inserted slides that deliberately create a pause or change of emphasis.

Scripting

Good presenters don't read from notes, just as actors don't read from their scripts. Effective communication arises from within the personality of the speaker and their authority to present specialist information. Some of the presenters who attend our courses like to have their talks written out on paper in case their words dry up. We try to discourage this because it limits their freedom of action, rather like being so reliant on the training wheels of a bicycle that they are unable to ride without them. However, there is nothing wrong with having visual cues on the slides to help you keep on track so long as they don't distract the audience.

Suggestions for slide construction

The following guide will help you to think about the most common issues arising in slide design. They are obvious points, but are so often missed by scientists who don't take the time to critically review their visual material in advance of presenting it. We hope that the clear guidelines and examples on the DVD-ROM will help to make this process as simple as possible.

> **!** The contents of the slide have to be legible; otherwise what is the point in showing it?

> **!** The contents should be relevant to what the speaker is discussing, and free of distracting features.

> **!** The key objective is to provide comprehensible information in the shortest possible time.

Slide background

DVD-ROM
Content: Slide background and themes

Most colour schemes use dark lines/text on a light background or vice versa. Blue backgrounds are often used for slideshows. The background colour doesn't have to be uniform; a slight gradient of intensity can work quite well. The idea is to keep the audience alert by using crisp, easy-to-read slides that don't depress by being gloomy (avoid mud-coloured backgrounds) or dazzle by being too flashy. PowerPoint offers many design themes that are attractive in an artistic sense, but generally unsuitable for scientific presentations. This is because they draw attention away from the information being presented. Background themes that sit behind the text and graphics can be a major distraction and should generally, but not always, be avoided. It is possible to use a background image to fill the whole screen to act as a theme. Text boxes and graphics can then be overlaid and removed as the talk progresses. This has been used for very effective talks on cosmology and particle physics; the background is mostly black, but dotted with dozens of colourful galaxies imaged by the Hubble Space Telescope. The speaker can then begin the presentation by immediately placing the subject matter (galaxy formation or the nature of elementary particles) within the context of the universe and its origins. The detailed material (equations and so on) is then added and removed as the talk progresses. Because this example has a mainly dark background, the material is presented on a pale background for maximum contrast.

Institutional or company design themes can intrude significantly, either as borders, or as logos displayed at the bottom right hand corner of each slide. The safest option is to avoid borders altogether and to keep the bottom logo at a size that is just legible. Alternatively the logo could be prominently displayed on the first slide and be absent in the rest.

Colour contrast

Technical presentations often have text, charts and diagrams with different-coloured lines. Use colours that give a high contrast against the slide background and avoid examples such as yellow lines on white (these happen). Some examples are shown on the DVD-ROM, but it is important to experiment for yourself and review the result when projected. Red is a very powerful colour, but you should be aware that an estimated 5–8% of men are red/green colour blind, therefore there is a need to use these particular colours carefully.

Text

DVD-ROM
Content: Fonts

Text and graphics must be clearly visible from the back of a large hall – size and contrast are important.

Use a sans serif font such as Arial. Serif fonts (such as Times New Roman) are used extensively for publication, but do not work well when projected on a slide. The font size (point) is usually a minimum of 24 for maximum impact in the largest conference rooms, but some legends to graphs or literature references may be smaller. Adjustments to text size can be made during final editing and review.

Graphics

Complex information is often better conveyed using graphics rather than text – remember the saying "a picture is worth a thousand words". Unfortunately, many presentations seem to consist of those thousand words written onto slides in long lists which the audience cannot possibly read in the available time. Text slides are often little more than written cues to help the presenter who is speaking without notes. Dealing with this to the satisfaction of both speaker and audience is one of the greatest challenges that you will have to meet during the preparation of your talk.

> **!** Learn to précis sentences that would normally be written out in full, if necessary adding them sequentially as builds (see Slide transitions, below).

Graphics offer an immediate solution to the problem of conveying information in a short period of time, but as with slide design, there must be a balance between legibility, impact and avoidance of annoying distraction. A highly complex diagram can make a point about the physical complexity of a system, but avoid the words: "you won't be able to read this, so I'll move on to the next slide"; it makes the inclusion of the slide seem pointless.

> **!** Use a title on each slide to summarise the information presented.

Sometimes non-scientific graphics can make a point, or just provide a planned break in the flow of the talk. Acknowledgement slides that have a picture of the speaker's institution or his/her co-workers are effective in this way, as is a humorous (but relevant) cartoon, but in this case allow plenty of time for the punch line to sink in!

> *One of our delegates used a cartoon to introduce some technical aspects of microscopy. The picture showed a caveman looking through a huge microscope-like contraption with a mammoth directly underneath – the caption read "I think it's a mammoth!" This neatly provided an introduction to the main theme along with a bit of light relief for the audience.*

GRAPHS AND CHARTS

> **DVD-ROM**
> Content: Figures, tables and graphs

Most scientific talks are concerned with research data obtained from laboratory experiments. The audience is not reading (or refereeing) a paper and hasn't the time to absorb anything other than the key points. Tables can be effective, but only if the text is easily legible and the key information highlighted, perhaps in a different colour. Long tables are not useful except in publications – process the data as graphs or charts instead. The latter must be clearly legible with all axes and legends clearly marked. The type of graph used will depend on the data and experimental design, but histograms and pie charts are often highly informative. Resist the temptation to show more than two graphs on the same slide at once; use slides sequentially instead.

ANIMATION

Scientific concepts can be very difficult to convey

DVD-ROM

Content: Builds, transitions and animations

rapidly, even to a specialist audience; animated graphics or movies can be a very powerful way of achieving this so long as they are not gratuitous or overdone. Animation using graphic objects to progressively build up complex systems or pathways is particularly useful. The diagram can be built up on the click of a mouse, or set to run automatically.

Be careful to check that animations and similar files will run on the computer provided for the conference or seminar and be prepared to do without them if there are technical problems.

SLIDE TRANSITIONS

These provide a smooth transition from one slide to

DVD-ROM

Content: Builds, transitions and animations

another. Many transitions are available (the dissolve transition works quite well), but only a few really seem to work without creating a jarring effect.

Transition effects are also useful for progressively introducing text that would be too much to take in all at once.

Final editing and revision

The final edits and revision can be done on any computer using the full screen page to run the slide show. Normally there will be minor text and layout changes, as well as checks for working animations and transitions.

Timing the talk is critical to avoid having to rush at the end, or not even complete the talk. PowerPoint has a facility for setting a fixed time for each slide so that the talk can be synchronised accordingly. It is also possible to use the *Rehearse Timings* feature to display the duration of each slide transition as well as the total time of the presentation.

It is very helpful to have access to a digital projector, since the slide show can look unfamiliar when enlarged. Colours can also be projected in a slightly different hue, so adjustments to these may need to be made by trial and error on the computer. When a presentation is projected in a large conference hall, the perspective of the slide content changes depending on the height and distance of the screen from the speaker. This can be very disorientating, so you should quickly run through the talk in the hall itself (perhaps in a break prior to the session) if possible.

4 Controlling nerves

"Relax. You're a famous author – no one expects you
to talk about anything other than yourself."

Many readers will refer to this chapter first. Nervousness before a talk is almost universal and is a problem that not only causes misery for the speaker, but also can ruin even a well-constructed presentation. This chapter will cover how nervousness shows and how to conceal it, using the adrenalin produced productively and not negatively.

Nervousness

> **!** "It's positive to be nervous, because is shows you're focused and ready, but you have to control the nerves rather than allow them to control you." (Pierluigi Collina, Soccer World Cup Final Referee).

We've all been there: the heart pounding, the ribcage barely able to contain it, the mouth dry, the palms sweaty and the head feeling like it will explode. This is all about performing in front of others, and scientific presentation is no exception. The reality is that you will always be nervous before presenting, whether it is a speech at a wedding, or a seminar to fellow scientists.

Nerves indicate that what you are about to do is important. For example, you don't (normally) get into such a state when talking to friends on the telephone or ordering a meal in a restaurant. Nerves can be used to your advantage, the resulting adrenalin rush propelling you forward. It's all a question of knowing how to conceal and control them.

Why are we nervous?

Understanding why you are nervous is the first step towards getting this state of mind under control. Almost all the reasons given by our course participants are linked to judgement by others. People do not want to look stupid and make a fool of themselves, or fail to answer questions at the end of the talk. There is a real fear of being judged by one's peers and seniors. The other reasons given for nervousness are linked to the act of presenting: worrying about drying up, not having enough information to fill the allotted time, feeling inadequate for the task and disliking being in the spotlight. Add on fear of failure and fear of the unknown and it's no wonder that the heart races faster!

How does nervousness show?

Nervousness shows in many ways and often you are not aware of how it is affecting your voice and body. Most people are not so good at spotting the flaws in their own presentation. This is revealed at our practical sessions where talks are videoed and the speakers can actually see how they come across when the video tape is replayed. Many have never realised that they have, for example, a nervous giggle or a tendency to look up, but having seen the evidence they can do something about it.

Not everyone does all of the following, but every one of these "nervous habits" has been observed in speakers from diverse backgrounds (head teachers and politicians for example).

FEET
A toe that taps constantly
Rocking backwards and forwards on balls of feet
Shifting weight from foot to foot
Walking from one end of room/stage to the other

Crossing one ankle over the other
Soft shoe shuffle.

HANDS
Gripped tightly, knuckles clenched, in front of body
Not still, i.e. wringing, twisting a ring
Gripping the lectern too tightly
Jingling coins in pockets
In pockets where the hands flap away so that the pockets look like the
    wings of a penguin
Spectacles constantly pushed back on to the nose
Constantly being run through hair
Tucked defensively across the chest
Attached to arms that wave around too much
Hands on hips.

VOICE
Lots of "ums" and "ers"
Words swallowed
Rapid speech with no pauses
Voice shakes
Voice goes higher
Mouth goes dry
Breathless speech because of shallow breathing
Nervous giggles.

EYES
Eyes fixed on the floor or ceiling
All eye contact avoided
Gaze fixed on just one solitary member of the audience
Blank stare that resembles a rabbit frozen in car headlights.

This long list of nervous traits can be seen frequently, but it does not help
you or your audience if you look nervous. The audience concentrates on
the nervousness and stops concentrating on what is being said. However,
it is the reality that you will be nervous, and it isn't necessarily a bad
thing so long as your nerves are channelled in the right direction.

A journalist wrote about a politician speaking at a conference:

> *This is a woman who simply cannot keep her hands to herself. It is*
> *impossible to concentrate on her views about the economic*
> *repercussions of monetary union while her hands are describing large*

circles, straight lines or little hoops. Every so often, she sticks them in her pockets, but even there they get the better of her, and she ends up flapping her jacket like a bird.

How to control nerves

There are simple, practical measures that can be adopted to conceal nerves and it is all about being in control.

Take control of your breathing

> **DVD-ROM**
> Example talk: Slides 3, 4, 8, 9

Take a few deep breaths and exhale slowly. Notice how you already feel more stable and centred. It is not necessary to breathe deeply all the time – indeed that would appear unnatural – but some good deep breaths before starting a presentation will help reduce the heart knocking against the ribcage. It also helps oxygen get to the brain and work with the adrenalin in a positive way to get you started.

The effect on the voice of proper breathing is noticeable. The voice won't shake and you will have enough breath to sustain your sentence. If the pitch of your voice has a tendency to go higher, the deep breath will bring down the pitch straight away. Good breathing means getting air deeper into the lungs. When frightened or nervous, people often breathe in a shallow way, with quick intakes of breath that barely reach the collarbone. When you have to talk on such breaths, the words cannot be projected well and everything comes out in a choppy and staccato manner. It is not satisfactory at all for a listening audience. So consciously breathe more deeply: it's like filling up the tank rather than trying to talk on empty.

Take control of your body

> **DVD-ROM**
> Example talk: Slides 1, 2, 3, 4, 10, 11

FEET

All those problems to do with feet can be eradicated by standing with your weight evenly distributed on both legs. This is also kind to the back and provides a comfortable standing position if you are talking for twenty minutes or so. It gives you stillness and a quiet sense of authority, just the right impression for a presentation.

HANDS

The easiest way to control hands is to have them loosely at your side or behind your back. This doesn't mean that the hands will always stay there as it is likely you will be operating images on a computer, holding a pointer or illustrating something with a gesture. Just remember to put your hands back in "neutral" (i.e. at your side or behind your back). Some presenters can look quite natural with hands in pockets but others can look sloppy and disrespectful. It's time to take a long look in the mirror and determine how you appear.

The value of eye contact

DVD-ROM
Example talk: Slides 1, 2, 5, 12, 13, 14

The importance of eye contact cannot be overestimated. Remember, you are not a radio programme or a textbook, you have an audience – everything goes better when you acknowledge it. Scan the audience, whether there are four in a boardroom or two hundred in a conference hall. If you dislike the idea of looking someone in the eye, look at their forehead. You will be creating the same effect as making actual eye contact. Never fix your gaze on one person, however friendly, smiling or nodding in agreement they may be. Pity the poor person trapped by your gaze and think of all the others who feel you don't want to communicate with them.

The most important methods for controlling nerves are summarised in the chart below. Also look at examples on the DVD-ROM of speakers revealing several nervous traits and then controlling them.

Breathing	The key to being in control – breathe deeply a few times before starting the presentation
Eyes	Make eye contact and scan the audience
Feet	Improve stance and stand with weight evenly distributed
Hands	Control hands. Have them at your sides or behind back
Arms	Avoid crossing arms over the chest – it looks defensive and aggressive and interferes with good breathing
Voice	Control voice shaking, pitch and jerky delivery by taking a few deep breaths before speaking
Dry mouth	Think of something that makes your mouth water

Too bored to talk?

DVD-ROM

Example talk: Slides 1, 2

One form of nervousness manifests itself in a very different way to those we have described already. This occurs when a speaker is so worried about presenting that they appear bored and disengaged and don't seem interested in communicating at all. The voice is flat and uninteresting and nothing in their research seems to excite them. The overall impression is one of couldn't care less. We know that is not the reality and that the curse of nerves is at work. Fixing breathing, stance and eye contact will all help, as will reading the chapter on "Voice" and associated DVD-ROM material. It is of course possible that you are genuinely bored with your material, perhaps after giving the same talk many times over; even if this is the case, you must be professional and overcome this boredom.

The value of a smile

DVD-ROM

Example talk: Slides 1, 2, 10, 11

A good atmosphere is created by rapport with the audience, and this must be established at the outset. Even before you utter a word, you must smile at the start of your presentation. Not a cheesy, insincere, white-teethed smile, but one that signals you want to be here and will enjoy imparting your information to your listeners. Smiling may be the last thing you feel like doing, but force yourself: if you do, the audience will pick up all the right signals about you being a confident and engaging speaker.

Communication is always two-way. You might be doing all the talking (except during questions), but you can still sense the mood of the audience and how they are reacting to you. If necessary, adjust your style to keep them attentive.

Starting off

When you start your talk at a conference or seminar, we strongly recommend that you learn your opening line – concentrating on that line will stop you thinking about yourself. What you actually say can vary according to circumstances. For example, you may introduce yourself and the organisation you represent, unless that has just been done for you. Sometimes a mildly humorous comment can break the ice – maybe a comment about your journey to the venue if anything noteworthy happened. If the audience has been following a theme covered by a series of talks, you could link your own to that theme: "You have heard about the role of X in Y, I'd now like to expand on this and introduce the role of Z."

It is not really feasible to learn a twenty-minute presentation by rote, as this could make it theatrical and forced. After all, you are using visual material that provides cues for the next part of the presentation. While you need to know where the presentation is going, you do not need to be word perfect.

The technique of visualisation can be of great help to some, while others see no benefit in it at all. It can help as preparation to visualise the room where you will be presenting, imagine yourself standing at the board table, or walking to the podium. Think about that confident stance and your introductory smile. Visualise the slides and the laser pointer you may be using. See yourself operating the computer to change the visual image. Imagine the scenario of being asked a question. This technique is really just another way of getting ready, of preparing, of not being fazed by a new experience. If it works for you, then that's great. If it makes you more nervous, then stick to the other practical advice given in this chapter.

If your presentation is part of a series of talks in a conference session, it can help to question another speaker prior to your own talk. This requires you to speak out, thereby drawing the attention of the audience to the voice that they are going to hear soon from the podium. This can be a very effective way of defusing anxiety in advance of your talk, so long as the question is relevant!

TO GET YOU STARTED
Confident stance
Smile
Learn opening line.

EXERCISES FOR BREATHING AND RELAXATION
Breathe deeply
Put your hands on the top part of the ribcage
Now breathe in and feel the ribcage expanding
Slowly exhale and repeat.

DVD-ROM
Exercises: 1, 2

To help you relax
Imitate a yawn
Hunch your shoulders up to your ears
Clench your fists
Release shoulders and fists
Repeat.

Other simple relaxing exercises
Clench and unclench your buttocks
Scrunch up your face and relax
Move your jaw from side to side
Shake your arms and hands
Roll shoulders back and then forwards.

Practical strategies to conceal and control nervousness

There are many strategies for this. Some require you to look at yourself and see what needs to be concealed. Others require you to think about the initial impression you make. If you can be videoed and analyse what you see, this will help you greatly. We know changes can happen, and quickly. At many of our sessions, the advice has been taken and young scientists have seen themselves on video looking confident and in control, whereas before, they did not look credible as speakers. It is true to say that most still felt intense nervousness inside, but they realised that this did not show and that they were definitely up to the task of presenting.

5 Voice

"Hey, I'd recognize your squeaky, high-pitched voice anytime."

A speaker with a monotonous voice will induce boredom in the audience, however interesting the data presented. This chapter will cover voice modulation, including the use of volume, pitch, tone and speed. We discuss the value of pausing and emphasis, and what to do if you dry up. There are several exercises to help your voice have clarity and variety.

Voice

> **DVD-ROM**
> Example talk: Slides 1, 2, 3, 4, 8, 9, 15, 16

Most of us have a fair idea of our appearance. We look in the mirror, use passport photos for travel documents and mark most enjoyable occasions with a picture. We may catch glimpses of ourselves on CCTV cameras in shopping malls, but very few of us have an idea of how we sound. It can come as a bigger shock to hear our voices than to see what we look like.

How would you describe your voice: is it deep, high, shrill, breathy, or like a loudhailer? Have you ever really listened? Have you enough breath to finish a longish sentence or do you speak in short, choppy sections? Are you naturally quiet with a voice that dips away at the end? Do you have a voice that is easy to listen to or is it, frankly, a bit of a challenge? Try listening to your voice objectively. Strange things can happen to it when you shift from conversing animatedly and naturally with your friends to being an isolated speaker. The natural rhythm and enthusiasm can disappear and you can sound flat, bored, rushed, as if you are reading everything.

The spirit of this book is practical and designed to help you make the best use of your communication skills. There is normally no physical impediment to how we speak; we just do not use what we have effectively enough. It is quite possible to alter your voice. Think of people who have eradicated all trace of an accent, like actors who can convince us that they are Scottish, Texan or cockney. This is a book for scientists, and the interest in the voice stretches to how you use it for your presentation – it has to be "fit for purpose".

It must be heard

First and foremost, a voice must be heard. There is little point in presenting if no one can hear what you are saying. Many people who have small, quiet voices are not breathing in the right way. In a formal environment, there is almost a risk of hyperventilating as the speaker struggles to project the words on diminishingly small breaths. Once again we come back to the importance of good breathing. It is possible to be overloud, and that can be uncomfortable for an audience to listen to. So, the golden rule is to be loud enough.

Mumbling

Many people mumble and don't articulate their words. While this does not matter in informal conversation, the consequences during a talk are much the same as not being heard at all. Often the reason for such sloppy speech is that people do not open their mouths sufficiently, they do not sound all the consonants of a word, and the sentence can fade away at the end. If you think this applies to you, then refer to the exercises that come later on in this chapter. These exercises are a sort of "mini work-out" for the voice. They will physically warm up your voice and increase muscular coordination.

Scientists use an enormous range of words that are rarely used outside the context of scientific research. The following words occurred in a six-minute session at one of our presentation skills sessions:

Elution
Adsorption
Extrude
Homologous
Proteomics
Desorption
Genomic
Agonist.

Apart from being struck by the scientists' definite advantage while playing "Scrabble", we noticed that these words were often pronounced in a rushed way and skimmed-over by the speaker. These specialist words must be practised so that each syllable is pronounced. It is also a good idea to pronounce them purposefully, in the same way that they would be marked by a highlighter if they were part of a written text.

Avoid being boring

The voice is like a musical instrument. It can be tuned and played. It is so easy to add variety. Here are a few ways in which it can be done.

> **!** "It don't mean a thing if it ain't got that swing." Duke Ellington

---

Pitch

This is about speaking higher or lower, about where you pitch your voice. A high-pitched voice will certainly gain attention but can be uncomfortable to listen to, while a low-pitched voice is generally associated with a position of authority but can be soporific. To find your natural pitch, you just need to hum. Then it is a question of consciously varying the pitch to add some music to your voice. Sometimes, people who do not enjoy public speaking tense up around the neck. This has the effect of stiffening vocal chords and making a speaker sound rigid and strangled. If this is happening to you, then you need to breathe properly and make a conscious effort to lower your pitch.

Tone

This is about how the sound can colour your voice. You can sound warm, engaging, shrill, soothing, worried, persuasive, knowing or bossy, for example, and it can all be conveyed by your voice. Experiment with tone. Try saying the word "yes" in all the ways listed above.

PRONOUNCE "YES"
Warmly
Sympathetically
Shrilly
Soothingly
Worriedly
Persuasively
Knowingly
Bossily.

Volume

Obviously your voice can be softer or louder. Extremes range from shouting to whispering, neither of which is greatly useful in a scientific presentation. We are not talking here of the "small shy" voice that needs correcting by proper breathing. We are talking here about consciously deciding to turn the volume up or turn it down. A judicious change in volume can prevent your voice becoming monotonous and boring to listen to. There is a problem with being overloud, and if you think this might apply to you, then ask a friend to listen to you and be honest with you. The phrase "loud and obnoxious" does not just come from nowhere!

The volume you need to use will depend on the size of the room in which you will be speaking and the availability of a microphone (see later). There is a big difference between an in-house presentation to five or six people and a hotel function room that can seat an audience of two hundred. Many people think their voice will not reach all two hundred and panic that they will not cope. The rule with any venue is to speak to the very last row of the audience, whether there are two rows, ten or thirty. Your voice will project to the back and be heard by all.

Speed

You can bring variety to your voice by changing tempo, by speaking faster or more slowly. You should aim for a comfortable speaking speed then consciously decide to alter the speed as you go along. A speaker who speaks slowly and deliberately for twenty minutes will bore everyone, and the audience will give up listening. The nervous speaker, who aims to get through the presentation as quickly as possible, will run all the words together without stopping to draw breath. This cannot be listened to for very long. "Detailedexaminationoftheresultsoftheexperimentsshow ... " does not appear to mean very much when it is printed, and it is just as meaningless when it is spoken in this way. At times, however, a phrase or two speeded up can give the audience a jolt and make them think an important point is coming. Try this sparingly.

Emphasis

Look through your presentation again, and decide which words would benefit from a natural emphasis. This is like taking a coloured highlighter pen to a text. When you have decided what the important words are, scientific or otherwise, make sure you give them added stress in your presentation. Try the following:

Peter's son is not working   Say this sentence, putting the appropriate emphasis on **one** particular word so that you come up with the meanings (1) to (4)

(1) Not Paul's son
(2) Not his father
(3) It is a fact
(4) Peter is lazy.

Enthusiasm

Most importantly of all, a voice can convey enthusiasm. And there is nothing more satisfying than a speaker who enjoys their subject and conveys this. Too often we have listened to speakers who lack enthusiasm, perhaps through nerves, and yet they love their subject and are

fascinated by their research findings. You only need to think enthusias-
tically for that to be conveyed through the tone of your voice.

Pausing

Never underestimate the value of a pause
as it gives the listener time to take on board

DVD–ROM
Example talk: Slides 5, 8, 9

the information you are giving. This is particularly relevant to scientific
presentations since they are very heavy on information. In other forms
of public speaking, the pause can be used for comic effect: it is the
basis of comic timing; or for dramatic effect: think of the oratory of
great politicians. Many speakers hate the idea of silence and think that
a pause will mean that they have lost their thread. Look at your material
once more and identify where there are changes of direction or subject
matter. All of these changes require a pause, and it can be quite a long
pause. The phrase "one Mississippi, two Mississippi, three Mississippi" is
well known as a device for counting down time, and the phrase takes
three seconds to say. So, you could silently say this in your head when a
pause in needed (and you would be in good company: John Wayne, the
American actor, reputedly used this technique). You could think of your
own "pause line" – "one ligand, two ligand, three ligand" perhaps?

! "The right word may be effective, but no word was ever as effective as
a rightly timed pause." Mark Twain, US novelist and humorist

A good exercise is to write out a paragraph or two of your talk, highlight
words which you think should be emphasised, and mark where you think
a pause should occur. For example:

! The term **lipid** comprises a diverse range of molecules [pause] and to
some extent is a catchall for relatively **water-insoluble** or **non-polar**
compounds of biological origin, including **waxes** [pause], **fatty acids**
[pause], fatty-acid derived **phospholipids** [pause], **sphingolipids**
[pause], **glycolipids** and **terpenoids** (e.g. **retinoids** and **steroids**)
[pause]. Some lipids are **linear aliphatic molecules**, while others have
ring structures [pause]. Some are **aromatic**, while others are not. Some
are **flexible**, while others are **rigid**.

Drying up

This is a major source of worry for the inexperienced speaker, and can sometimes explain why you are so reluctant to use pauses. You worry that if you stop, you might not be able to start again. It can happen to us all, at any point in a presentation, but it is not the end of the world, and the audience will have no idea you have dried up unless you let them know. To the listener, it will just appear as a pause and one which helps them to absorb all you are telling them.

TAKE A DEEP BREATH

This will send oxygen to the brain, and help you be in control again. You have visual aids that will provide a cue for you and all will be well as long as you do not panic.

NEVER APOLOGISE

The audience cannot read your mind. They do not know the sequence for your presentation. Never say "Sorry, I've lost my place, I've lost my thread, Oh sorry, I think I'm making a mess of this."

The goal of your presentation is to make people listen. It's not just what you say, but how you say it. By using a voice that is audible, clear and varied, you help your audience to listen. Now it is time to tape-record yourself, play back the tape and listen to how you sound. See if there are any adjustments you can make, using some of the suggestions above. Try some of the exercises that are listed below. And remember to convey the enthusiasm you feel for your work and research to those who have come to listen.

Exercises for the voice

> **DVD-ROM**
> Exercises: 3, 4, 5, 6, 7

There are whole courses and countless books containing exercises dedicated to the voice. We have selected exercises that will make a difference to you and help with your scientific presentations. However it is not our aim to produce a voice that can deliver "King Lear" eight times a week. There are no exercises that involve you lying on the floor or speaking with a cork in your mouth; that would be over the top for what you need and might scare you off! All the exercises will help with clarity and variety and are for practising at home, rather than just before giving a talk.

> **!** Work on vowels. This helps clarity
> **A, e, i, o, u**
>
> Say each vowel with the inflection going up
> Say each vowel with the inflection going down
> Say each one with the inflection going up and then down
> Say each one with the inflection going down and then up.

> **!** Making you open your mouth
>
> Pronounce the vowels a, e, i, o, u, yawning when you pronounce each one.

> **!** Finding your pitch
>
> Find your natural pitch by saying "mmm"
> This helps if you think your voice has a tendency to go high
> This helps to relax tense neck muscles.

> **!** Improving your pitch
>
> Say the following several times, making your voice go up or down, depending on whether you need to higher or lower your voice:
>
> "I can make my voice go higher and higher / lower and lower."

> **!** Tongue twisters
> **Making you use your mouth and voice**
>
> Repeat the following as fast and as many times as possible before the sense falls apart:
>
> Peggy Babcock
> Red lorry, yellow lorry
> The tip of the tongue, the teeth and the lips
> A proper cup of coffee in a copper coffee pot
> She sells sea shells on the sea shore
> Round the ragged rocks the ragged rascal ran.

6 Delivery

"I know so much that I don't know where to begin."

This section on delivery is where you reinforce the development of your own style. You are not trying to be a clone of anyone else. You may admire a particular speaker, but it is best to be yourself and work with your characteristics and personality. If you are naturally quiet and dignified, don't try to be loud and theatrical. We will discuss the relative merits of different postures as well as the effectiveness of using gesture and humour. There is a section on using a microphone and laser pointer.

> **!** "There are always three speeches for every one you actually gave. The one you practised, the one you gave, and the one you wish you gave."
> Dale Carnegie

We have now arrived at the point where nerves are under control, there is effective use of the voice, a stance that shows confidence, and plenty of eye contact. As far as delivery of a presentation goes, you are on the right track.

There are, however, many other practical aspects to consider. You should have controlled all those signs that displayed nervousness (listed in Chapter 4). If you threw your arms around like windmills, or paced the floor, this should now have stopped. But do not go to the opposite extreme; it will look equally odd if you stand like a plank of wood. A rigid posture will induce boredom, so there is a place for movement and gesture in your presentation **as long as it is controlled.**

Where you stand

You should always aim to face the audience. You shouldn't face the visual images you are presenting and you should never stand right in front of what you want the audience to see. This sounds very basic, but the number of times we have seen speakers face the screen or board, and obscure the very images they wish us to see, means that it is worth stressing. You do not need to scrutinise your slides in the lecture room, you should have done this while preparing your talk, and know them inside out (beware of the danger of using colleagues' slides that you do not know well). If you follow advice elsewhere in this book, you will be working with a manageable number of visual images that provide cues for you to go on. So there is no need for you to be glued to the images you are projecting.

You may want to point out things, and we suggest you stand to one side of the screen and turn your body through approximately 45 degrees if you wish to point something out. And are you right or left handed? Is it going to be easier for you to point something out by choosing to be on one side rather than another? Crossing your arm over your body to point out something looks awkward; and means that you will not be as clear as you would like because your body is obscuring the screen.

You should stand up, even when presenting to a small number of people. This immediately gives you control of the situation as well as gravitas. It indicates that the talk is properly thought out and not casually presented.

It is not a good idea to hide behind a podium, but we realise that this happens. Make sure you are not gripping the side of the podium too tightly.

Far too often there are lectures on paintings in London's National Gallery with the lecturer standing right in front of the painting being discussed. This has meant: (a) I cannot see the painting and (b) I cannot hear what the lecturer is saying. The speaker might be brilliant but there is no way of knowing!

Pointing

The most common gesture is point-ing. We have watched all manner of

DVD-ROM
Example talk: Slides 6, 7, 8, 9, 10

ineffective pointing over the years: this ranges from the "one-second stab" with one finger (nowhere near the image projected), to the waving of arms where you would imagine an alarm was being sounded. Pointing should always be open, not across your body. And you must **point for long enough** so that your audience can follow your indication. It is probably good practice to point for longer than you think is necessary. The audience is always a few seconds behind you, processing what they have just heard and seen.

Laser pointer

Laser pointers can be a very effective tool but they need to be handled with care or they will not help your presentation. As with not pointing for long enough with the hand, so it is with laser pointers: a quick flash of the red light is no help at all – blink and you miss it. There are also those who cannot keep the laser pointer still and produce a hypnotic swirl of red circles that mesmerises the audience and distracts it from what it is supposed to be looking at. Remember to switch the beam off when you are not using the pointer; you could inadvertently shine that beam into the eyes of the audience – a far from pleasant experience.

For those who are rather self-conscious about what to do with their hands in a presentation, holding the laser pointer with both hands can be a solution. It looks quite natural. However, resist the temptation to grip it with all your might or to twist it and fiddle with it. If you have really shaky hands and find it difficult to keep the gadget still, then do not use it. The essential point is to keep the use of the laser pointer under control.

!	Keep it under control
	Point for long enough
	Avoid creating red circles
	Switch beam off when not using.

Gestures

DVD-ROM

Example talk: Slides 12, 13, 14

While you must control your stance, you should not look stiff and wooden. An animated speaker always communicates better, and using gestures is as much a part of this animation as using a varied and enthusiastic voice.

There are endless ways of using your arms and hands to help clarify the points you are making, with pointing being just one. Think about what you wish to convey and see if you can create a visual analogy.

Here are some examples of gestures that we have seen used to good effect:

Point being made	Accompanying gesture
Number of points/reasons to be made	Holding up corresponding number of fingers
Emphasising a point	Hitting back of the hand into the palm of the other hand
Interlinking of molecules etc.	Interlinking fingers
Graph of performance with one out-performing another	Raising hands horizontally, one going higher than the other
Spiral movement/tendency	Creating a spiral with finger
Wavy movement/tendency	Creating a wave with hand
Flat and calm movement	Hands moving evenly across a pretend surface
Balancing up two sides of an argument	Using the right hand for one side, the left hand for the other (the phrase "on the one hand ... on the other" can be used literally)

As a London guide, I have said on thousands of occasions that Tower Bridge opens in the middle. This has led to as many queries as to which bit actually moves. Some think the road lifts up all in one piece, while others think part of the bridge swings round. The easiest way for me to explain the bascule motion of the world-famous bridge is with a gesture – hands meeting horizontally, and then swinging to vertical, just like the bridge. It is amazing that such a small gesture solves so much for the questioner!

Using props

Complex technical material can be simplified to convey the key message in a number of ways. We have already mentioned using analogy to familiar events in Chapter 2. Physical props can help audiences by providing a three-dimensional view of a scientific phenomenon, and can be very powerful. They also have the benefit of drawing the audience's attention towards the speaker and away from the slides.

> *Props can certainly make an impact on an audience. A parasitologist in an American university used to have a jar of rubber worms on the podium and then deliver a lecture to his students on a series of gruesome infections with visual material to match. At the end of the lecture he would throw the worms into the unsuspecting and, by now, queasy audience, thereby causing mass panic. Students used to come up to him for months afterwards with a worm in hand, so it was certainly memorable.*

Using a microphone

"Great! OK, this time I want you to sound taller, and let me hear a little more hair."

It is highly likely that you will have to use a microphone if speaking in a venue larger than an average room, so it is worth running through the different types that you might encounter.

> **!** Fixed microphone
> Hand-held microphone
> Hands-free microphone.

The fixed microphone must be set at an appropriate height and kept at a constant distance from your face.

It is vital that you do not turn away from the microphone while you are speaking as the sound will fade every time you look at your slides.

The hand-held microphone has the advantage of allowing you to move around, but it might be awkward if you have slides to change with only one hand free. It is also important that the microphone rests on your chin or is just below the lips so that the sound from your mouth passes over the top of the microphone.

DVD-ROM
Example talk: Before speaking – attaching a microphone

The hands-free microphone (sometimes called a lavalier) has a transmitter which is worn on the body. The microphone can be worn round the neck or clipped onto clothing and allows you to move around freely. If you know you will be using this device, choose your clothes so that there is somewhere for the microphone and the transmitter to be fitted! If you have to attach the microphone to your lapel yourself, make sure you face away from the audience while doing this. In this way, no one will notice if your hands are shaking or if you fumble while trying to clip the thing on. In your own time, and when the microphone is attached and switched on, turn to the audience ready to begin.

Whichever type of microphone is used, it is always a good idea to try it out before the presentation. Even if that is not possible, you still must understand the room setup, talk to the technician and establish who changes the slides and whether to use a laser pointer.

In general, speaking close to the microphone gives a voice warmth, an immediate presence and a fuller sound. The further away the voice is from the microphone, the thinner, reedier and more distant you will sound. Speak clearly into the microphone and never shout. Take care not to stand below an amplifier as this could lead to feedback.

Remember that microphones can pick up all sorts of sounds and comments, so be careful what you say once you have finished – that aside may be picked up by everyone in the conference room.

> *CNN anchor Kyra Phillips went to the bathroom with her microphone still on and made many unflattering comments about her family. This couldn't happen to a scientist could it?*

Humour

Humour, whether verbal or visual, makes an audience relax and be more receptive to what you are saying. We would not advocate telling jokes unless you are a very experienced speaker and are used to "working" your audiences (and sometimes the subject matter makes this impossible). However, we firmly believe that you should look at where a little humour could add to your presentation. We have already mentioned using cartoons as natural breaks in presentations and you will have noticed in this book several used in this way. With all humour, however, time must be allowed for the punch line or the visual equivalent to sink in. Give your audience time to digest it.

The cosmologist Stephen Hawking is a good example of someone who takes his science extremely seriously, but is not afraid to have a bit of fun at his own expense by appearing in "The Simpsons" TV show. Talking science with Homer Simpson over a few beers, Hawking declares "Your theory of a donut-shaped universe is intriguing . . . I might have to steal it." The point here is that a bit of self modesty can endear you to an audience without undermining your authority to present original science.

> *Sometimes the opportunity to introduce humour comes unexpectedly in the middle of a presentation. A Japanese speaker heard a phone ringing at the back of the conference hall and, without missing a beat, said "Ah, more data!"*

Beginning and ending a presentation

DVD-ROM Example talk: Slides 1, 2, 15, 16

Good speakers make an entrance with confidence and energy. Remember, you are on show from the moment you step onto the stage, not from the moment you start your presentation. Make sure the impression you are creating is the right one. Your appearance is important, and, rightly or wrongly, people judge you by it.

Perhaps when you have made a name for yourself as a scientist, you will be able to appear as you want. Until then, gain confidence from being appropriately dressed for the occasion.

> *Appropriate dress can vary according to the conference. Some winter conferences in the US are held at ski resorts, so the early afternoon speakers are often dressed in ski suits ready to take off for the slopes at the first opportunity.*

Good speakers let you know when they have finished – the presentation does not just peter out. Remember to have a strong exit line, one that encapsulates your "take-home message". The matter of timing has been dealt with elsewhere in the book, but never be in a position where you have to rush your ending. Every speaker should be able to summarise the content in about two or three well-constructed sentences. If time is running away with you, remember the summary and concentrate on your conclusion.

Practising your presentation

> **!** "It usually takes me more than three weeks to prepare a good impromptu speech." Mark Twain

Never underestimate the value of rehearsing and practising your presentation. When you are still relatively inexperienced at presenting, it is not enough to go through it in your head and think everything will go well, you must say the presentation out loud. As mentioned before, you should borrow a digital projector and go through the talk exactly as if it were the real thing. You must also check timings either the old fashioned way with a clock, or by using the facilities in PowerPoint. You may want to tape what you say or get a friend to listen to you. In this way, you will get used to the sound of your voice as a presenter and record a true time for the presentation. The maxim "fail to prepare, prepare to fail" applies to all presentations, including scientific ones.

It is useful to know your word count. Many professional speakers know that they speak 100 words a minute, while BBC newsreaders average 120 words a minute. A good rule of thumb is that you will actually take half as long again to present. So, 1000 words may represent ten minutes while practising at home, but will represent almost fifteen minutes when in a formal setting.

With practice, your presentations should move forward in the following way:

> **!** Unconscious incompetence
> Conscious incompetence
> Conscious competence
> Unconscious competence

Finally, ask yourself this question: "Would I enjoy my own presentation?" If you do, it will come over in your talk. If you don't, maybe others won't either.

7 Science and the English language

"You seem familiar, yet somehow strange – are you by any chance Canadian?"

It is a daunting task to present in a language that is not your mother tongue. This chapter provides guidance on bringing maximum clarity to your presentation through appropriate voice control and visual aids. This will also be useful for native English speakers since they often think they speak English better than their non-native counterparts. This isn't necessarily the case. In fact, non-native speakers from different countries and cultures often understand each other more easily than they do the native speaker.

> **!** "The language of science is broken English." Anon

At the start of the twenty-first century, a conservative estimate of the number of speakers who are competent in English is 1.5 billion people. That's a quarter of the world's population, with English-speaking countries represented in every continent, and with over seventy countries having English as an official language.

Any discussion of why and when the English language became the global language, whether this has roots in economic, political or cultural power, is outside the scope of this book. But for the foreseeable future, English is the language you are most likely to be presenting in – English has become the language of science. A toxicology conference, for example, may take place in Egypt, the speakers coming from Norway, Singapore or Turkey, but the conference will normally use English as the principal language.

International English is sometimes referred to as "Offshore English". This can be described as a modification of Standard English that is designed to be readily comprehensible to everyone, regardless of their country of origin. Both native and non-native speakers must modify their English for presentation purposes in order to achieve maximum communication with their audience.

> *If, as an English speaker, you do not think this applies to you, then consider the following: Korean Airlines awarded a lucrative contract for flight simulators to a French supplier rather than an English one because the French company's negotiators spoke clearer and more comprehensible English that was readily understood by the Koreans.*

Implications for the non-native speaker

> **DVD-ROM**
> Example Talk: Slides 6, 7, 10, 11

The aim of this publication is practical.

It will not attempt to teach you English as a foreign language, but it will give helpful advice to improve the clarity and effectiveness of your presentation. We do, however appreciate that it is still a daunting task to present in a language that is not your mother tongue.

USING VISUAL AIDS

We covered the use of visual aids (in the form of PowerPoint) in Chapter 3. The emphasis was on using text and images to complement the spoken words, but not to hijack them.

Where the speaker has limited English vocabulary and grammar, however, the slides should be designed to convey the key message to an audience almost independently of the speaker. Handouts (given out only at the end of the talk) can be a powerful way of getting your message across, if practicable.

Sometimes a speaker's strong accent can mask the meaning of a word or phrase, so the best plan is to display key words and phrases to make the meaning unequivocal.

There may also be a case for keeping the number of slides quite low to allow the audience extra time to read the material. Don't underestimate the value of colour and images to make your point. Finally, you should take extra care to make the summary and conclusions slides clear and concise.

CREATING A CLEARER SOUND

The rhythm of the language

You may write the language perfectly, be grammatical and select vocabulary carefully, but that does not mean it is easy to listen to. The more you can reproduce the natural rhythms, the correct emphasis, the rising and falling intonations in a language the better, and this you achieve by getting your ear attuned to the "music" of the language.

One way of doing this is to actively listen to formal spoken English. The more you can do this the better, although we don't expect you to speak like the Queen of England. Being English ourselves, we would recommend BBC news bulletins, maybe picked up on Internet radio or television. Other English-speaking countries will of course have their equivalents that can be used instead, but watch out for pronunciation. Some countries broadcast programmes in English that is spoken with a very heavy accent, making it difficult for a non-English speaker (and by extension your audience) to comprehend.

Pause frequently

Pause after a particular unit of meaning, such as a sentence or phrase. This is not the same as speaking slowly. In fact, speaking slowly can be monotonous and sometimes sound a touch patronising. Build in the slowness with pausing.

Keep sentences short and simple
Aim for simplified sentence construction, avoiding too many subordinate clauses or additional phrases in a sentence. Keep the tense of the verb basic. Put a new idea in a new sentence.

Pronunciation and articulation
This is an aspect of English that is very difficult to master as there are so many exceptions to the rules. If you know a native speaker, ask them to listen and put right any obvious mispronunciation. Sound every consonant. It's not necessary to do this in ordinary speech, but for presentations, this will make you clearer. It may also slow you down a bit. If you don't open your mouth enough, you will not be able to articulate properly. Try some of the tongue twisters (see the chapter on "Voice"). For further practice, and a little bit of fun, say out loud the cautionary tales by Hilaire Belloc: "Henry King" and "The Microbe" which are printed at the end of this chapter. These will help with rhythm and pronunciation, and will challenge you to open your mouth.

Implications for the native speaker

> **!** "English as spoken by natives can be baffling to foreigners."
> Roland Gribbe

For those whose mother tongue is English, part of the problem is that the speaker does not believe there is a problem, after all it's their language. But English speakers can get lazy; they need to examine their use of English and how they articulate. They often think they speak English better than their non-native counterparts, but this does not always lead to comprehension. In fact, non-native speakers from different countries and cultures often understand each other more easily than they do the native speaker.

At a business conference of the European sector of a large Japanese car company, retailers from Japan, the Czech Republic, Germany, the UK, France and Italy all gave presentations in English. Where necessary, they were helped by a teleprompter that shaded words to be emphasised and underlined where stress in the word fell naturally. Arrows pointed upwards to indicate when to alter the inflection of the voice. All delivered clear presentations with pauses and relevant gestures, outlining the growth and potential of the company in their various countries, except one, who came from England. He believed he was using his native language best because he was a native speaker. But the reverse was the case: He spoke too fast and did not enunciate sufficiently. He was the least intelligible of all the presenters and there was noticeable shuffling and fidgeting from the audience while he spoke.

The following will help you examine your use of English and understand the difficulties that can arise in comprehension for non-native speakers.

AVOID FALSE FRIENDS

Many English words and phrases look and sound very similar to words in other languages, whereas the reality is that these words mean something very different. It is worth looking again at your presentation to see if there could be ways in which words could be misidentified. For example, "to table", in the context of a meeting, can mean "to raise for consideration" or "to suspend from consideration" depending on whether you are meeting in Britain or the United States.

AVOID PHRASAL VERBS

A phrasal verb is a combination of a verb and a particle (usually a preposition or an adverb) that changes the meaning to make a new verb. These are very frequent in the English language and are very difficult for non-native speakers to master. If this all sounds very complicated, you probably use several per sentence and do not realise you are using them! The following list using just one verb stem will give you an idea of what language learners are up against. If there is an alternative, aim to choose a verb that is not phrasal and therefore unambiguous.

Phrasal verb	Alternative verb
To put away	To return to the proper place
To put by	To save for later use
To put off	To postpone, delay
To put out	To extinguish
To put over	To convey
To put up with	To tolerate
To put upon	To impose on, to overburden

AVOID COLLOQUIAL IDIOMS

An idiom is a figure of speech that often adds colour to the language, but can be a source of incomprehension and lead to serious misunderstanding. It is wise to consciously avoid a phrase that you know will not be understood outside your country.

Here are just a few idioms that if looked at from a logical rather than a linguistic viewpoint would be baffling:

To beat about the bush
By the skin of one's teeth
To cost an arm and a leg
To hit the ground running
To keep one's nose to the grindstone
To paper over the cracks.

Although the English language is colourful and idiomatic, the best scientific presentations for native and non-native audiences keep it simple and literal.

Exercise in articulation

Recite the following as clearly as you can, and savour the fun of the verse!

Henry King

The Chief Defect of Henry King
Was chewing little bits of String.
At last he swallowed some which tied
Itself in ugly Knots inside.
Physicians of the Utmost Fame
Were called at once; but when they came
They answered, as they took their Fees,
"There is no Cure for this Disease.
Henry will very soon be dead."
His parents stood about his Bed
Lamenting his Untimely Death,
When Henry, with his Latest Breath,
Cried "Oh, my Friends, be warned by me,
That Breakfast, Dinner, Lunch, and Tea
Are all the Human Frame requires ... "
With that, the Wretched Child expires.

The Microbe

DVD-ROM
Exercises: Improving
articulation poem

> The microbe is so very small
> You cannot make him out at all,
> But many sanguine people hope
> To see him through a microscope.
> His jointed tongue that lies beneath
> A hundred curious rows of teeth;
> His seven tufted tails with lots
> Of lovely pink and purple spots,
> On each of which a pattern stands,
> Composed of forty separate bands;
> His eyebrows of a tender green;
> All these have never yet been seen–
> But Scientists, who ought to know,
> Assure us that is must be so ...
> Oh! Let us never, never doubt
> What nobody is sure about!
>
> *Hilaire Belloc*

8 Handling questions

"That's an excellent prescreened question, but before I give you my stock answer I'd like to try to disarm everyone with a carefully rehearsed joke."

Often the nervous speaker is also nervous of being asked questions and doesn't like them. This chapter will provide practical help on deciding when to take questions, and make sure that they have been heard correctly and answered in a way that keeps all listeners interested.

Questions form a significant part of any scientific presentation. It is the ideal way to allow for expansion on a topic and confirms that the presentation is two-way. But those who are nervous about giving a presentation are also often nervous about taking questions. Always remember that the scientific research that you have undertaken is **your** research and only you can really have the answers to points raised by your presentation. If you have prepared well, kept your nerves in check (see previous chapters) and then followed our guide for answering, you will come to find this part of your presentation one of the most enjoyable. The question and answer session is not an occasion to fear, but a real opportunity.

Why do we like or dislike questions?

When conducting practical sessions, we always ask the delegates whether they like questions or not. The replies are always divided into a "yes" and a "no" camp. Those who like questions usually do so because it indicates many things about both the speaker and the audience: the attendees have been listening; they trust the speaker sufficiently to ask for expansion; and they believe a worthwhile answer will be given. As a form of two-way communication, the asking of questions involves everyone in the meeting, and there is much satisfaction and pride in providing a considered answer.

Those who dislike questions are often worried that they will not know the answer and do not want to lose face in front of their colleagues. They feel their knowledge will be challenged. But there are other reasons expressed for this dislike of questions. The question can interrupt the speaker's carefully planned flow or may pre-empt a point further in the presentation, resulting in the loss of precious minutes. And then there are those questions that seem designed to trick the speaker, that feel like a superior testing a junior, or a competitor fishing for as yet unpublished material.

> *The British Museum in London published a book called "Behind the Scenes" containing a list of questions that have been asked over the years at the Information Desk. Some would definitely prove challenging to answer!*
>
> *Do you have Jesus' manger here? How did they know it was BC? Is your exhibition on ancient-Egyptian gas masks still on? Do you have a knitting pattern for a Viking jumper? I would like to make an appointment to see the Museum's eminent archaeologist, Indiana Jones. Elizabeth Lewington, Visitor Services, remarks, "I am always keen to impress on new staff that the greatest asset ... is not necessarily to know the answer, but to know where the answer can be found."*

Controlling when questions are asked

There is normally a fixed time for questions at the end of a conference presentation, so it is rare for anyone to interrupt during the talk. You therefore have automatic control over when questions will be asked. This may not be the case in a seminar, despite the custom of reserving ten to fifteen minutes for questions at the end. You may be interrupted in mid flow, so answer briefly unless you are going to address the question later on, in which case say so. If questioners persist, make it clear that questions are welcome at the end. The important point is that you are in control and you set the time for questions.

Do you worry that there is **silence** after you have asked for questions? You probably think it is longer than it really is, like a pause in your presentation. The audience is always a few seconds behind the speaker, processing what has been heard, and needs time to think. It can take a little time to move from being a listener to being a questioner. Avoid looking agitated or concerned; it may be that there are no questions!

The following practical tips will help you through the expected question session by giving you techniques for answering in an effective way.

Guide for answering

Look interested and show pleasure when the question is asked. Some speakers look horrified when a question is asked and convey anxiety without realising it.

Listen to the question you are being asked. This may seem obvious advice, but how often do you anticipate the question to find out that this is not what is being asked at all?

Repeat the question, either verbatim if short, or paraphrase somewhat if long. There are good reasons for this. Firstly, you are making sure that everyone at the meeting or conference hears the question and is involved. Secondly, you are making sure that you understand the question that is being asked (and if you haven't, the questioner may well interject). Finally, you have given yourself a little extra time to think about the answer. So often, a nervous speaker will immediately resort to saying he/she doesn't know the answer when in fact he/she does. It is nerves that take over. If you can delay that moment, you will find that, of course, you know the answer.

Answer briefly, or as concisely and succinctly as your topic allows. Avoid giving another presentation.

! Guide to answering questions

Show pleasure
Listen to question
Repeat question
Answer briefly.

Anticipate questions

What questions do you think could be asked that relate to your presentation? Being prepared for your presentation also means being prepared for questions. You will not be able to think of everything that might be asked, but working out half a dozen or so potential questions and how you might answer them will always be time well spent.

Dealing with difficult questions and questioners

In the world of science, what would be considered a difficult question? Questions that interrupt, pre-empt, cause you to lose your thread or are just inconvenient are irritating, but might not be classed as difficult. However, questions that are clearly silly or irrelevant can be more difficult to deal with. Show-off, silly or trick questions tell you more about the questioner than the subject of your presentation, while what is considered a provocative, personal, offensive or confrontational question may vary from one scientist to the next.

Questioners may not express the query clearly or may be difficult to understand. They may simply wish to make a statement, and not ask a question at all, or they may wish to dominate the proceedings. Under these circumstances it is good policy never to cause embarrassment to your questioner, even if they embarrass you. It may be that the questioner has not been listening and asks a question that you have already addressed in your presentation. It is not helpful to remind the questioner of this, so treat the question as you would any other, that is repeat the question and answer as best you can. This applies equally to questioners who appear provocative to you; they almost always appear provocative to the rest of the attendees. Repeating the question will highlight the provocation and calmly answering it will give you the moral high ground – the audience will be on your side (unless of course you have been excessively provocative in your talk!).

If you feel a competitor wants proprietary information or research data that are not yet available, it is quite permissible to refuse to answer by replying that it is not yet published.

If you consider the questioner is asking something with a very narrow viewpoint that will not engage the rest of the audience, offer to discuss this outside the session. Similarly, it is wise not to get into a dialogue with one questioner as this also could result in the audience losing concentration. As speaker, you always have the last word. Reinforce your take-home message after the last question, and in this way you will re-establish what you want the audience to remember.

> *Scientific arguments can become quite heated, but are normally kept within the bounds of civilised behaviour. Not so with two successful immunologists who got into a full-scale brawl at the conference podium. The reader should refer to books on self defence to deal with this eventuality.*

When you don't know the answer

The question to which you do not know the answer is probably the one you fear the most. You may have prepared thoroughly and be on top of your material but sometimes you really do not know the answer. There is only one course of action . . . Do not lose your cool, do not panic, don't get angry or be rude. Never lie if you don't know. You might throw the question to the audience – someone may know the answer – or you may offer to find out or suggest where someone might find it.

> *Making an educated guess at a question is possible, but carries risks. A tourist guide was taking her group to Chartwell, the country home of Sir Winston Churchill. In the grounds of the house, a plant with leaves resembling giant rhubarb grows by the side of the pond. The guide anticipated that the group would comment on such extravagant foliage and that they would want to know its botanical name. Try as she might, she could not recall it, and when asked, she found herself saying, "It's something like syphilis. While you are in the house, I shall find out for you." She made enquiries at the shop to discover that the plant's name was Gunnera.*

Question types	Action
Time losing, pre-emptive, interruptive	Set a time for questions
Irrelevant, inconvenient	Set a time for questions
Silly, show-off, trick	Remember the value of repeating the question
Competitive	You need not give information that is not yet published
Personal	You may be politely evasive if the question crosses your personal line
Provocative, rude	Remember the value of repeating the question. The audience will be on your side, and you do not have to answer
When you don't know the answer	Never make it up

Examples

DVD–ROM

Example talk: Answering questions 1 and 2

9 How did it go?

"You can't argue with success."

> **!** "All the great speakers were bad speakers first." Ralph Waldo Emerson

> Few books on this subject consider "How did it go?" All advice is geared to preparing and presenting the material. It's as if, the moment you have finished presenting, it is all over. It can take months to prepare and moments to deliver. We believe that evaluation after the talk is very useful and will help you with presenting the next talk.

Take a moment to reflect on how your presentation went. If you think it was successful, several of the following may have happened: the audience listened and showed appreciation, whether by direct thanks or with applause; relevant questions were asked; there was contact and networking at the break-out sessions; and later on, invitations to speak elsewhere.

If you felt things had not gone well, perhaps you noticed the attendees were talking amongst themselves, or yawning or sleeping. Perhaps you

noticed a distinct lack of response and the questions asked seemed irrelevant. Nobody sought you out at the break-out sessions, and worst of
all, some got up and left while you were speaking.

Sometimes the negative points are not a result of your presentation, but
an indication that the participants have, for example, travelled from far
away and are jetlagged.

Reviewing your slides

Were there too many? Did they all work? Did one slide lead to confusion
rather than to clarity? Did a slide provide the cue that you needed? Were
the colours used effective? Was the typeface clear enough? If you think
a slight change is needed, make it now. If you leave it until you present
this topic again, you may well have forgotten and your slides will not
be aiding your presentation.

Timing

Did you run to time? Did you run out of time and rush towards the end?
Make a note of how long this presentation actually took. Write down the
timing and then consider if you are happy with this or if some tweaking
of the material is required. Do it now, as you will not remember in a
week's time.

Humour

**Did the audience appreciate your use of humour? Did you give time
for the humour to be appreciated? Did you get an audience reaction
that you weren't expecting?**

The key message

Was it stressed? Did you think you managed to get it across strongly
enough? Was it what you ended with?

Questions

It is worth evaluating the questions you were asked. They might have
arisen because of:

- Lack of clarity on your part
- Too much detail on your part
- An illogical argument
- Inability to include everything in the time allotted.

By evaluating what you have been asked, you can decide if the answer you gave should have been part of the presentation; whether you could have spoken more clearly and precisely; or whether the question took the conference into a whole new realm that no speaker could have predicted. You are then in a position to change aspects of the presentation or realise that it went well and could lead to other areas of the topic.

Conference setup

Did it all go as planned? Was the laptop/slide projector/microphone as you wanted? Did you have appropriate technical help? Could you run through things in advance of your presentation? Are you already making mental notes on what to check next time?

Find opportunities to practise

It cannot be stressed often enough that practice really does make a difference. If you have spent time carefully preparing your talk, think where else you might be able to give this talk. Don't just wait for someone to ask you to present, make the opportunities yourself.

Opt for professional help

The authors of this book run regular tailor-made courses on presentation skills for scientists. An objective assessment can often be just the input you require and make all the difference to your presentation skills. These courses are put together by ScienceInform.

Conference checklist

Contains list of key points for last minute check-over.

Length of talk (slide number)
Slides confusing/too complex?
Colours/fonts
Animations, transitions all working correctly
Run through voice/breathing exercises
Be in control of microphone, either hand-held or clip-on
Memorise first line
Consciously suppress any body movement if over active, or animate
    if inactive
Pauses and voice modulation
Punchy ending and include acknowledgements (or at beginning)
Welcome/repeat questions.

Further reading

There are many books on general presentation techniques, a few of which are included in this list. We have also listed books dealing specifically with scientific presentation that provide useful background material. We particularly recommend the books by Vernon Booth and Robert Anholt.

General presentation

Jo Billingham, Giving Presentations, Oxford University Press, Oxford 2003.

David Crystal, English as a Global Language, Cambridge University Press, Cambridge 2003.

Patsy McCarthy and Caroline Hatcher, Presentation Skills: The Essential Guide for Students, SAGE Publications Ltd, London 2002.

Anne Nicholls, How to Master Public Speaking, How to Books Ltd, Plymouth UK 1995.

Cristina Stuart, Speak for Yourself, Piatkus Books Ltd, London 2000.

Scientific presentation

Robert R. H. Anholt, Dazzle 'em with Style, W. H. Freeman and Company, New York 1994.

Vernon Booth, Communicating in Science, Cambridge University Press, Cambridge 1993.

Scott Morgan and Barrett Whitener, Speaking About Science, Cambridge University Press, Cambridge 2006.

D. Eric Walters and Gale Climenson Walters, Scientists Must Speak, Routledge, London 2002.

Training company websites

Scientific presentation skills training companies:

UK based: ScienceInform Ltd, www.scienceinform.com.

USA based (Washington DC): Premiere Public Speaking, www.premierepublicspeaking.com/.

Index

acknowledgements, 11, 20
adrenalin, xi, 23
afraid of making a bad impression, 4
Albert Einstein, 4
analogy, 9, 10, 43
animation, 10, 21
articulation, 32
audience, 1, 4, 14, 26, 28, 29, 41, 45, 57, 61
    audience expectation, 1
    knowledge of, 4
    lack of concentration, 3, 62
    particular needs, 2, 5
    specialist, 3, 4, 9
    target audience, 2
    with a political agenda, 5

body control, 26
    feet, 26, 27
    hands, 25, 26, 27, 41
    how to stand, 26
    stance, 26, 40
breathing, 26, 27, 32
    effect on voice, 34
    exercises, 29
British Museum, 56
builds, 21

cartoons, 12, 20, 45
colloquial idioms, 53
colour, 20, 22
colour blind, 19
colour schemes, 18
company logos, 19
conclusion, 10, 11
conference checklist, 64
conference set up, 63
conference theme, 9
content, xi, 14
    data, xi, 5, 10, 11

drying up, 37
DVD-ROM, viii, xii, 18, 19, 20, 21, 26, 27, 28, 29, 36, 37, 42,

electronic media, 15
emphasis, 35
English language, 49, 52, 53
    International/Offshore, 49
    non-native English speakers, 49, 51
    the language of science, 49
enthusiasm, 35
evaluation, 61
exercises, 29, 37
    articulation, 53
    breathing, 29
    relaxation, 29
    voice, 33, 37
eye contact, 27

flowchart, xii
font, 19
    font size, 19
    legibility, 11
    sans serif, 19
    serif, 19

gestures, 42
graphics, 10, 18, 19, 20
graphs, 21

handouts, 50
hands. *See* body control
Higgs theory, 8
Hilaire Belloc, 51, 54
    Henry King, 53
    The Microbe, 54
histograms, 21
Homer Simpson, 45
Hubble Space Telescope, 18
humour, 12, 45, 62

internal lab meetings, 7
International English, 49
    Offshore English, 49

key message, 8, 9, 10, 11, 15, 16, 43, 46, 59, 62
keynote speech, 7, 11

Large Hadron Collider, 8
laser pointer, 29, 41
lymphocyte signalling, 12

microphones, 44
microscopy, 20
motivations, x

nervousness, 5, 23
    how nervousness shows, 23, 24
    looking bored, 27, 28
    nervous traits, 24
    questions, 55
    techniques for controlling, 26, 29,
        30
    why we are nervous, 23

opening line, 27, 28

pausing, 35, 36, 50
personality, 17, 39
phrasal verbs, 52
pie charts, 21
pointing, 40, 41
PowerPoint, 7, 14, 15, 17, 18, 21
    "death by PowerPoint", 14
practising, 46, 63
preparation, 5, 6, 22, 29
presentation, 2, 5, 7, 19, 37, 55
    as a selling exercise, 2
    beginning, 3, 45
    crafting the presentation, 8
    ending, 46
    evaluating, 61
    logical sequence, 9
    over-complex presentation, 3
    planning, 6
    structure, 9
    summarising the content, 8,
        46
    tailoring the presentation, 2
pronunciation, 33, 50, 51
props, 43

questions, 29, 55
    answering questions, 57
    anticipating questions, 58
    difficult/awkward, 58
    evaluating, 62

repeating the question, 57
    when to take questions, 55, 56
    when you do not know the answer,
        59

rapport, 28
    smiling, 27, 28
relaxation exercises, 29
Richard Feynman, 4
rubber worms, 43

scientific presentations, i
    definition, x
    logical sequence, 9
slides, 10, 16, 17
    colour contrast, 19
    conclusion slide, 11
    definition of, 7
    design theme, 17
    final editing, 21
    number used in a talk, 7
    reviewing, 19, 62
    slide background, 18
    slide construction, 11, 18
    slide transitions, 17, 21
    text slides, 19
speaker appearance, xi, 44,
        45
Stephen Hawking, 45
storyboarding, 16
storytelling, 11
summary, 10

tables, 14, 20
take-home message See key message
timing, 1, 6, 21, 46, 62
    finishing the talk early, 10
tongue twisters, 37, 51

using the DVD-ROM, xii

visual cues, 17, 29
visual material, 13, 14, 18
    digital projector, 22
    electronic media, 15
    flipchart, 7
    overhead projector, 7
    PowerPoint, 14
    projector carousel, 14

visualisation, 29
voice, 26, 27, 31, 32
    articulation, 51
    audibility, 32
    clarity, 37
    exercises, 33, 37
    lack of clarity, 32

pitch, 26, 33, 37
speed, 35
tone, 33
variety, 33
volume, 34

word count, 46